Lo Locked

Together Dreaming ~ Awake

By

Silviya Ilieva Dimitrova

To Me and Him. To Us.

As to all Twin Flames out there, who are fearlessly flying towards
THE FLAME.

LOVE LOCKED is a collection of 22 real life inspired, magical renderings.

They will open your heart to the existence of pure love.

That on a deeper- Soul level.

Shifting you mind away from all physical and leading you towards the unseen- felt.

Capturing your spirit in an instant.

Silviya is well known for her ability to express her deepest feelings with an incomparable ease and in the most hard hitting way possible.

Within this treasury of musings, she has beautifully depicted the complexities of a Twin Flame bond.

So much so, that the reader will most certainly sense the impact this one love has had on her.

CONTENTS

ACKNOWLEDGMENTS i

1. *Mischievous ~ The Night* 1

2. *Pure Is Love*..2

3. *Silent ~ His Inner Riot*..4

4. *Flying Tandem*...6

5. *Steadfast Universe*...7

6. *Surrender*..8

7. *Love Locked: Together Dreaming ~ Awake*......................10

8. *Divine Trip*...14

9. *Two Hearts*...16

10. *Elusive Worlds* 18

11. *Whole* 20

12. *Blossom & Dusk* 22

13. *Luscious ~ His Soul* 23

14. *Again*...24

15. *One Flame*...26

16. *This Love* 28

17. *Find Me* 29

18. *Complete*..30

19. *Tingling Chills*..32

20. *Dancing On Ice*...33

21. *On Fire* 34

22. *Mystery Of Love* 36

ABOUT THE AUTHOR 37

ACKNOWLEDGMENTS

I would like to thank one very special person, for being the inspiration behind LOVE LOCKED.
His name is Stanimir K.

I am grateful for our paths crossing the way they did.
For nothing was ever planned.
For it was meant.

Travelling solo to a city and country I've never visited was scary and exciting, all at once.
Yet it was magic, because I met you.

For feeling so deeply connected to someone I was meeting for the very first time is elusive.
For experiencing such pure, raw and sincere emotions so suddenly is rare.
I love you.

You happen to be my Muse.
Thank you for being.

I'm embracing all felt unseen.
Until we meet again.

I would also like to thank my Publishing team at Kindle Publishing UK for surrendering their time and positive energy and helping me make this book a reality.
Finally I would like to express my unfeigned gratitude to the Universal Master and our Creator for gifting me with the ability to express myself with so much love, light, positivity and conviction.

1. Mischievous

The Night

Let's dance
~ beneath the moon light
Let's play
~ each other find
Let's twine
~ divinely
Because
~ mischievous the night

2. *Pure Is Love*

The MIND will call it FOOLISHNESS.
The SOUL
~ SURRENDER

In GIVING IN there's nothing FOOLISH.

We're simply moving with the FLOW ...
There's NO RESISTANCE.

For MIRK needs GLOW
~ NOT DARKNESS

For EGO is in agony already
~ needs NO AFFLICTION
MELTS under ACCEPTANCE, CUSTODY and WARMTH.

For when we TRULY LOVE SOMEONE
~ we give them LOVE

For LOVE is LIGHT and PEACE and FREEDOM.

In LOVE the TWO are ONE.

The INNER'S as the OUTER.
The BELLOW is as ABOVE.

THINKING'S FOOLISH
~ comes from EGO

SURRENDER'S INNOCENCE.
And PURE is LOVE

3. Silent

His Inner Riot

You whispered...
~ shhhh
Silent your inner riot.

Ok, I'll mute my senses
~ rewire
Simply be.
Here
~ suspire

I'll let the feeling burn
~ feed the fire

Then set my soul free
~ out the ashes
Flying inspired

4. Flying Tandem

Two bodies...
In one soul unified.

Two spirits
~ free
Each Other purifying.

Apart and together...

Life simplifying.
Love solidifying.

Remotely
~ in tandem flying

5. Steadfast Universe

Love's here ...
In the shape of broken glass.

Lost and just as fragile
~ the outcast

Love's within us all.
And all around
~ forever lasting

LOVE'S OUR STEADFAST UNIVERSE.

Let's swim in it
~ TOGETHER

As ONE
~ IMMERSE

6. Surrender

Her love eternal is and timeless.

His soul craves space
~ for self reflection
Silence.

She wrote
"I love you ... I surrender ..."

No single letter back
~ nor render

Yet innocent, sincere ...
~ strong
The steel.

That tender heart within her whispered softly:
"Let no one rob you of your light and zeal."

Now
~ shhhhht
Mute the noise.
Be still.

KEEP SPREADING LOVE AND ALWAYS DAZZLE
~ REMAIN GENTEEL

7. Love Locked

Together Dreaming ~ Awake

Friday at work.
Sleepless night
Last-minute packing, wine and coffee.
Pre-flight
Bathing...
Releasing LOVE
~ LIGHT beaming
Travelling towards the felt
~ unknown
Yet down to Earth
~ not dreaming
Landing solo...
~ vulnerable, fearless, excited
Adamant to find her way around it...
Curious and self-reliant.
Trusting
~ this soulful inner riot
She wondered, feeling lost and dazed
~ somewhat confused
Yet jolly and unfazed.
Then, close to 10am she typed
"Hey, I've arrived,
yet never felt so lost..."
And it was "sent"
~ she had so far survived
Yet was exhausted.
Felt hot, her inner voice appeared

~ both, fearful and delighted
"Whatever did I do?! Ohh dear."

Wild Fire within her
~ unseen
Ignited.
Next, his airplane touched ground
~ response had reached her phone
And timely.
The vibes were gentle
~ not intense
Magnetic tale was to commence.
Somewhat woolly, vague, yet restless.
She chose to freshen up and dress.
Then go, explore this city.
Exert
~ not waste
Her verve, her infinite avidity and zest.
Late afternoon
~ still fidgety and tense
Scouting town
~ disposing fear
With intent.
Time swiftly passed...
They chatted
~ tryst was set
ITALIAN
~ the style
At last, they met.
Two hearts were wildly racing.
Extremely nervous
~ each other facing
The night was ludic.
Their souls on fire
~ at its peak
Warmly embracing.
Both looking sleek.

A bond, so strong.
Lustrous
~ their eyes
Entranced dancing...
Later he whispered gently, caressing her face
~ coming clean
"You are beautiful... wow, how soft is your skin..."
Talking for hours
Not rushing...
~ pacing
Together
~ the daylight greeting
Sadness with Faith replacing.
Sharing breakfast, coffee and spiced ginger shots.
Their aim is to catch
the 11.18am train.
Walking.
Reaching the station on time
~ both looking blurry
and strained
Jumping on swiftly.
Him, throwing jokes.
Both dashingly laughing
~ high on the LOVE drug
Anxious to part
~ full of beans
Two spirits
~ twined
Resembling teens.
Dreading the pressing rupture soon pending...
Holding hands
~ tightly crossed
She tiptoes to kiss him.
He looks in her eyes and sighs "Thank you"
On escalator
~ moving
Towards his gate.
He was to take off first.

Her flight was due three hours later.
Two people
~ apart
In tandem breathing.
One SOUL divided.
Blinding LIGHT beaming.
Remarkable LOVE
~ LOCKED
By FEAR and past distress...
No beginning defined and no end...
By all means, no goodbyes either
~ Laters baby
I'll see you soon... then

Who can tell what the two main characters were truly feeling?!
I can
~ because this is my story
Not passing fancy...
I saw it through its very coda.
And it was real.
It was romantic.
It was thrilling
~ worth it
Chancy

8. Divine Trip

Book of adventure
~ her life
Some colourful pages gone missing
~ ripped
Her feelings, not once ~ examined
And closely.
Her beliefs
~ questioned
FLIPPED.
Testing ~ her path
Yet all the way worth it.
Because wild ~ her soul
From fear stripped.
Her name is LOVE.
She is light, free and happy.
Devine is her trip

9. Two Hearts

Two HEARTS
~ pounding
Back to back.
United.
As a PACT.

An inner fight and yes
~ insane resistance

We care.
We love.
We fear.
We're coming close…
We're drifting…

Because
~ electrifying
These emotions.
Because
~ our spirit's nudge
Persistent.

Despite the distance
~ existing
Within us
~ both
As all around.

Elusive, yet emotive
~ the fierce locomotion
Intoxicating
~ placid
Risky

10. Elusive Worlds

Surreal, how identical their inner worlds appeared
~ elusive

Her soul felt both elated and frightened...

Because
~ projecting

Yet she chose to embrace the unseen
~ felt

Because
~ MAGIC
Its POWERS

11. *Whole*

Seek the SOUL
~ WITHIN
HEAL those parts of you that hurt
~ FEEL them

Accept SELF completely.
Let all pain go.

Have FAITH and know
~ FIRST
We must go through the distance
~ TOGETHER
Allow LOVE.

Unite
~ when ready
As ONE
~ BEAT
Become WHOLE.

We are the centre of our world.
When the centre is affected, everything around the centre is.
The way OUT is IN.
Be ONE.
Be WHOLE.
MIND – BODY – SOUL

12. Blossom & Dusk

It was a sunny afternoon...
She held her own soul's hand...
Then asked her to get up, move and dance...

Suddenly her LIGHT beamed with such intensity, that even the
grey cloud she was trapped in started dancing...
Following in her footsteps
~ shifting
Sprinkling teardrops...
Cleansing her sphere.
Planting more seeds of love
~ within her
Then kindly showing her how to nourish them.

Because dusk loved blossom.
Because blossom loved dusk.

Because united
~ the twine
A pact.
Beaming brighter
~ together

That's a fact

13. Luscious ~ His Soul

Alluring...
~ within
And out.
His gentle toughness
~ tricksy
So endearing...
Honest
~ maybe not enough with Self
Sensual, attractive
~ too caring
Trusting, curious and bendy.
Cautious
~ faithful and daring
Lucid
~ his eyes
Emotive, sincere...
Just like the SUN
~ brightly glaring

14. Again

Early February ...

Sunday
~ noon

She gazed at him and whispered
~ yearning

Laters baby ...
See you soon then ...

Despondent he posed the question
~ WHEN

Late summer ...
It will be AUGUST
~ she responded

It will be WARM and SUNNY
~ ZEN

Both now fondly smiled,
For knowing
~ there will always be AGAIN

15. One Flame

Two spirits
~ yearning
No longer sane...
Each at its point
~ stuck
BOTH
~ wildly running
Towards ONE FLAME.

Mighty
~ the gravity
Because ONE FLAME

16. This Love

This love makes my heart beat.
It rules my inner world.
It multiplies my power.
It pumps my blood
~ runs deep
It makes me blossom
~ like a flower
This love heights makes me reach
~ eternity
Space further sky above us.
It burns like fire
~ gives me chills
Is everything our soul desires

17. Find Me

Let's trust this inner feeling
~ blindly
Attune with what's to come
~ divinely
Surrender to the flow, run
~ wildly
Impact our world
~ profoundly
When time is right we'll twine.
And timely.
First fly, discover Self.
Then find me.

Hey, hey Twin Flame, you are her brightest mirror...
She
~ yours

18. Complete

Performing
~ in charge
On fire...
~ burning

Feeling hot
~ roasting
With eyes scanning.
Looking thirsty.

Suppressing emotions.
Fighting weakened resistance.
Disturbed...
~ bursting with love
Dying to kiss her.

Descrying a figure
~ wavering
Enraptured, he beckoned...
She was there in a beat.

Both exhaled...
~ grateful
Embracing the heat.

At last together
~ at ease
For nothing was missing.
And all was complete

19. Tingling Chills

Tingling chills overload...
Fit to pause thinking of one another
~ NOT
Love caressed
~ each morning
Rising.
Because their eyes
~ the spies
Explicit are and tender
~ wise
Trusting their psyche's deepest cries
~ not rolling dice
For ONE they are...
Yet flowing free
~ enticed
Him and Her
~ BOTH
Know.
Her soul's his home
~ his safest place
to go
As Her and Him
~ BOTH
Know.
His soul's her home
~ her safest place to go

Because both so gutsy, steely, so relentless...

20. Dancing On Ice

Rapture shaken.
No.
Not forsaken
~ free
Awaken.
With love bursting.
Moving forward
In faith
~ trusting
Somewhat overtaken
~ not lusting
Spreading Light.
Active
~ in motion
Not rusting.
Faithful, determined.
Dancing on ice
~ adjusting
Always happy
~ elated
Adventure seeking.
Gently
~ thrusting
Blissfully burning like Fire.
Daring, yet tender
~ merriment thirsty

21. On Fire

Let's wipe these shades of grey
~ to clear our skyline
Splash sunny rays.
Come over
~ lay your head on my chest
With me
~ for me
Suspire.
And please
~ no more thorny tests
Because this heart for two is beating.
Sizzling
~ restlessly
On fire.

22. Mystery Of Love

There is so much beauty within the mystery.
Unveiling it
~ patiently
Purifying our inner world.
Shedding history.
Awakening
~ step by step
Feeling LOVE.
Deeply.
~ Hello Victory

ABOUT THE AUTHOR

Silviya I. Dimitrova is a naturally gifted storyteller and poetess and the author behind *FRAGILE STEEL ~ The Mellifluous Zing of My "Ear To Hear"*, an uplifting collection of powerful contemporary poetry, which was her debut.

She is an established influencer and voice within the hospitality industry, having published three articles at Carbon Free Dining, sharing her knowledge with the next generation of hospitality professionals.

Bulgarian by birth and based in London, England, since March 2001, she is a warm-hearted free spirit, who sees the beauty and light in everyone, everything and all.

She is an artist, love propagator, blogger, daring traveller and dreamer.

Above all else she is one kind and gutsy, positive believer.

You can visit her online at:

Instagram @silv_at_walkbesideme
Facebook @walkbesidesilv

Printed in Great Britain
by Amazon

45768802R00026